B. Z. NIDITCH

# EVERYTHING EVERYWHERE

**COVER PHOTOGRAPHY**
SARAH KATHARINA KAYSS

**MANAGING EDITOR**
WILLIAM JAMES LINDBERG

# *EVERYTHING EVERYWHERE*

Penhead Press Chapbook Series #4
First Print Book Edition July 2015
ISBN: 978-0-9887938-5-9

## Copyright © 2015 by B.Z. Niditch

This book was formatted, edited, and published by Penhead Press.

Special thanks to Denise Flanagan for taking B.Z. Niditch's photo displayed in the "About the Author" section.

Penhead Press
Willamina, Oregon
2012

**PENHEAD PRESS**
PO Box 115, Willamina, Oregon, 97396-0115
www.penhead-press.com

# C O N T E N T S

## J A N U A R Y

## F E B R U A R Y

# JANUARY

## *WAITING*

Waiting for
magnetic

sunshine
on deck

the joker
   meditates
under
the sound system

when a sudden rain
like    pawns
on the chessboard

invades
liquid solitude

sings
its vaporous solo

over a  ditch water
river of sensation

on our trio's  recital,
jazz opens
in an open space

and flesh murmurs,

my sax is ready

a firestorm
dissolves
conversations.

## RECOGNITION NO.2

Shock waves by the sea
of language to enter all channels
as futurist voices : listen for a swim
and a swan lake washes
a lost shroud in the river,
let the old clothed icons go
by a new green sap of lime trees
translated in a flash bulb,
art on a silver age's paper.

## JANUARY'S 3RD OFFERING

Away from bird nests
and blood baths
of hidden urges
and peripheral illusions
in our fugitive century
artists as only memory in
purges of our kick start day
in accusatory darkness
out of passion for remembrance
we survive another January Third
along a converse of borders
when our time as knotted papers
is posted on headstones
with obituary promises,
suspended as prison diaries
over unarmed screens,
(both film and computer)
relocated in past histories
unaware(on the defensive)
of a mishap risk of identities
from cliff notes and sheets

poets refuse to be banned
from our Republic's virtue
like any family of Platonic
patrons in retrospect and web
we ask to cease questioning
any asylum backgrounds
as masks for gestures
with discretion on yellow pages
on wrestled consciences
over watch lists of stamped
go through promises
of verbal barricades,
vast bureaucracies
feeling like Kafka and Kafka
(like unnoticed exiles)
we still live on Socratic grounds.

## AN EXPERIMENT

Janus gated by doors
in a second day of rain
illuminates the city's voice
heightened by exhaust furies
of auto's immune traffic
scattered glances direct me
to wild reflections from bones
under solar mammoths
on sunshine topped snow
rushing hours in avenues
to u turn the century
soon silence props up curiosity
at the opined murmurs of critics
from academic appointed dead dog-
tired factional languages
and third- hand irony,
we ask for experimental forms,
as cars pass by on lunar inclines
us as a stoned Sisyphus
presides to locate my recollections
brushing rocks down side hills

wanting to take short cuts
with sibilant sirens of creativity.

## ANOTHER EXPERIMENT

On frozen grounds
in kindled northern lights
shadowing owls
along geometric trees
from my ex camera
over street-wise lamps
(as January first carries
the snow whispered prophecy
in an experimental new year)
from an inconsiderate globe
in its hungry horse -trading
and two- faced survival
              in my mind's eye
(living alone, as a pack animal
slips away)
turning a tone poem memory
as a fragile hair taken comb
by an unfinished mirror
erases my initialed name
unbending lapses of locution
on the new alembic calendar.

## AT AN ART THEATER (JANUARY 9TH)

In a cinematic verse
at the first screening
holding onto French bread
from a sustained hunger
facing the Bay side of the city
on an art theater poster
eyeing "Stolen Kisses."

## Second Hand Stall

At a used bookstore
with two centuries of reading
already well-consumed
impatient for any ink- wise
ratiocination curled by
new light's dilated visions
of uncensored approval
over the walled high shelves
inspection ventures
by a penniless alleyway
with every impulse
to bury oneself to study
the Masters, by volumes hiding
to face columns of language
as a neon gold butterfly
netted in a defaced reading
as a Gothic margin ambushes me
by shaping time
in sink with verse lines
yet unaware (of the signature
of the love letter inside)

in animate Swedish
of arbitrary magnetism,
from a lit-crit commentary,1999
on "Cries and Whispers"
in an audited film class
of melancholic Bergman.

## PLACATING SLOGANS

In perpetual motion
creative lights flash energy
in unfaltering single time
to the tongue stretching
dawn, owning its existence
sky-written under city walls
hand warmed graffiti
up twenty-one scrappers.

## THE JANUARY 10TH COPING

Obdurate days
by a red eye age of silver
turns over you
to mahogany
and brass rings
denying to shape
the marble or clay
without a suspicious energy
in your tangerine jeans
working 24/7
to nullify a make-shift divorce
between art
and the abstraction
in the maladroit sentence
of your designed conviction
by road house portraits
you draw out the past
from sterile nostalgia
choosing a sculpture
of praise.

## JANUARY 15ᵀᴴ EXPERIMENT

Expecting no complaint
in my sound proof studio
living in a Hamlet's frozen face
gazes from a familiar window
a writer who still
carries a music case
with numinous blindfolds
augmented to ripened tones,
my lambent fingers
play a recondite soprano sax
to the operatic Carmen
who waves me on
as a narcotized funeral
in a surrendered sun
passes by a column
highlighted by a jazz band
visiting from New Orleans.

## LAMENTATIONS

Let's blame Aphrodite
when night surprises
your echoes settle
from breast to breast

The moon is feverish
to lock light in
hoodwinked by fate
the flesh tears at love

Indebted goddess
to an unarmed power
where fruit and music
jumble up paradise

among sleepless blankets
rinds, winds, gardens
tasting elixirs
of good fortune.

# FEBRUARY

# FEBRUARY 1ST DIARY, NO. 1

Bolting loneliness
near my vagabond vase
found in war time
by an orphaned child
stolen from thieves
and collaborators
painted in Mondrian orange
with reincarnated cold water
and dying jonquils
expecting a bunch to live
in her hair.

## FEBRUARY 4TH ART'S PROPOSAL

Shutting off A.M. news
reports before breakfast
of warring piped in factions
poly- sci heads
with sports and rock mayhem
pitching their elation
and commentary language
while I in a fulcrum's blank verse
do not forget the postmodern
as Odysseus' ship mate
never ages (in my art's passport)
life handpicks our soul like Pan
in unwritten seasons on deck.

## VALENTINE'S DAY

Sent out to my better half
in transience by cliff notes
of a no return love letter
of my translator
enveloped diaphanously
by an opened up avant-garde
no returned address
feeling an aimless amnesia
by reading your diary over
in a risible human eye
by the mountain ranges
where we once hid our photos
marked on stone tablets
by discarded grief
(confusing a, i, e, u,
in a matter of speech)
half-crazed like the larks
transferred by your
lost ski mask(discovered)
after your faceless accident
holding up time by paths

by rocky anemones
with instructions
to open this P.O. box for 2014.

## RECOGNITION No. 3

Blame the stars of silence
for the despair not the sea bird
undoing the ports of call
we caress symbiotic unreason
for omitted French love dreams
as no words: only this poet
by passes the king's English
for this vagabond's
Villon's invocation.

# THE THAW

Writers return
  from the Arctic snow
    the last descant
 of dissident past,
Fyodor,
the Decembrist past
    catches up
on a tragic black book
 seeking a sun's requiem.

## ON STANLEY BURNSHAW STREET

Somewhere between
Russian Dreams
and American know how
changing errata
of old matter locations
heavy weights carry
on the way of a political
phosphorescent dada red
on these winter nights
bearded as stubble,
those day bed times slept
in your first loves
of Rublev and troubled notes
gambled away
paint slides down (returning tips
from Rockefeller dimes
converted from rubles)
on cat's eye platforms
you spoke against fascism
by understated stars and crosses

behind windowpanes on Burnshaw St.
(a visionary knows it all)
wrapping a poem in cellophane
what coexistence is a loss
of underestimated crimes
not felt from the populists
even a Pound of flesh
demanding from language
a plum from Stevens
in a freshly skinned membrane
neglected from a separate
tongue and mouth,
let's be even handed
or double jointed at the hip
of your uncollected ninety years
getting even for a crumb
of this rejected voice,
keep on as what is lovely
the juice flows, next hour.

## *LOVE'S SELF DECEPTIONS*

When I journeyed
to Balbec searching
for wisdom
from Marcel Proust
to seek his grounds
for finding signs for love
heightened by the springs
of the countryside
far away other professors
    and student bodies
driven from the Eiffel Tower
cafes and tourist traps
              to find his secret
of what will remain after us,
it wasn't affairs
of business or sated times
which will collapse
it was in art
that you believed

and realizing it (like a holograph
                    on puffs of clouds)
was no longer deceived.

# MARCH

## THE MARCH EXPERIMENT

Awaken to build another tower
quivering like windmills,
words are never motionless
like green luminosity
on Mount Helena
stretching to the sky's dust
(a solar flare still resonant
off the obsidian volcano.)

## EXPECTATIONS (FOR TOMAS TRANSTRÖMER)

The trees cold as footsteps
alive as phantoms
of early music
when in amazement
March sky covers dawn
from pale first light
covering lichen and moss fields
after snow kisses
ungloved hands
once frozen in the sun
and open tundra
of omen or memory
fooling no one
in a vertical dare
near the green sea
between fjords
where house boats tremble
from the islands
to surface in the thaw
of landscapes

and life jackets
swaying gingerly
in the crevices
not forgotten
since climbing
mountain, tree, caverns
with woolen socks
pushing your weight
to host beach friends
who visit to play
under the galaxy
harmonic undertones
of experimental spheres.

## *A DIMENSIONAL BODY*

A work-out of dark print
falling from classical words
leaving us with myths,
thankful for comprehension
of a nature not departing
like centaurs in a dream
without double-minded
scores to unsettle
between beast
and the next man or woman
choosing the pro creative
salient masks to put on
not chafing at Virgil's past,
for beauty is not far away
from the ancients but lie
with us in blanket verse
over my sleepless head
and rolls as film clips
for the next installment.

# WANTING

Wanting these letters
to be alive as flares
in a desert rose patch
burning out a patch
of my roseate experiment
in a language the root holds
not to be underestimated
in arid times
by consciences
alive by wellsprings
of creative juices.

## IDES OF MARCH

Brutus, all Mr. Perfect
and well meaning
kills off Caesar
yet the locust of revenge
too strong for a history
plays on open-mouthed
guts of knives
words exalting the deed
in a melancholic speech
when mouths are muzzled
in street-wise astonishment
of a Roman revenge
Venus guides his fate
like Mars and Jupiter
in peacetime or war
and we in as back corner
of a spotty flattered world
do not know what occasion
when the stars arrange
its thoughtless letters

to banish a language poet
in a post modern universe
walking by the Capitol.

## MARCH 17TH

Listening to the piano
of Glenn Gould
playing Alban Berg's sonata
my body floats
in a proxy variation
when diminished time
drifts in the space
of an encounter
between bent fingers
up the sleeves
of the century's
contrapuntal double
voices of genius.

## MARCH 25TH

A recollection
of fractured phrases
gives signs
away from the past
yet always expecting
a peripheral vision
to embolden us against
any accusatory power
of reactionary interference
we will continue
with our words woven
like string theory
in spite of splitting obstacles
on the magnetic pole,
our quantum staying power
looming with enthusiasm
in projected geometric lines
knowing the day's redundancy
cannot entrap our space
from any drop shot language

in any egress of a foul
no matter what dryad
or wood nymph
hides in an adjoining forest
by the trunks of trees
our Muse, purged
of all absent translations
will offer a prophetic tongue
in phonemes of sound
to carry our dialect
intertwined as woodwinds
in a jazz quartet
to every century's notes.

## MARCH 27TH

Waves rise on the Missouri
in gyrations informing T.S.
of shore bird voices
as early morning swimmers
with St. Louis sun outside
his sound proof studio
with quick imperative notes
subsiding in young
Eliot's mind's eye
in full retreat he's plunged
without prevarication
to dive without interference
into the Muse's fore-play
eclipsed by tunnel-vision.

## CIRCLING

Bearded in wild flowers
unbuttoned as a statue
once sure footed Achilles
covered with moss
in a latitude with a logos
of his friends dead in war
forgetting all knee capped
lengths in his metaphor's footage
praises in decrees of flattering
once with thick handshakes
now his body build forever
bandages him forever.

## MARCH 28TH

Radar crossing
all lines
in lost postcards
letters and prints
like the Derain portrait
bought and sold
by the Vichy regime's
gendarmes in puppet shows
on street-wise France
some had taken you
as a collaborator
during your Occupation
when you were hiding
like francs in art pockets
while others were hiding
behind Parisian walls
for their hungry lives,
after the resistance
we located your print

in another painter's studio
short changed by history.

## *Speaking Outside Time*

Speaking outside time
and space
in abstraction's depths
of a simulacrum
in fear of a sustained oblivion
at a last year's
yellow book's recall
at an auction
which follows light streams
of a artist's drawing us
to the rebus of intention
in cover shrouds of canvas
waiting for an exhibit
photographed by sunshine
carried on barker's shoulders
in shrink-wrap blue film
spliced by the producer
trembling from amnesia
in a century's loose
monograph of time

of an alternative encounter
in anticipation of variables
by caliginous dark rooms
on a back city street
where still life's works
are oversold.

## *End Of March*

No chance
of a late counterpoint
letter of correspondence
a sad saxophone
troubles me
as if the solo cadenza
meant to light up
my sound proof studio
with all classical garb
is put away with Flaubert
Poe and Baudelaire on
the fireplace
no quarrel with me
if we still believe
in art's second chances
caressing a phone
with no one on line
nothing is spared
not even French bread
at three A.M.

my bare foot
catching a splinter
remembering the missive
of threatened suicide
when taking this apartment
lying under the floorboard
daring mortality,
perhaps Coltrane on radio
in his blindings note
over the motionless table
will release me
from tonight's emergency
as the fish tank blinks
with its own dementia
or read the funny parts
of last week's Times.

## *AT AN EXTENSION*

I held on, trying my hand
with the faintest sound
on my sax
sounding on fearful floorboards
contorted like conversation
forged from parental storms
with crabbed lean fingers
filled with house dust pages
weighed and tapered
by miles of absence.

# APRIL

## MY APRIL FOOL'S DAY

Dim last night's music
with premonitions
of spasms of recordings
blaring out its needle
unfeeling by the wood stove
as a bicycled man
drifting with tattoos
with handlebars for arms
and veteran smart talk
asks to borrow sugar
from my empty kitchen
locating a coupon
not yet perishable
in the rain.

## SUMMONED

Summoned by once wintry
burnished sunlight
not out of shame
of a weekend runaway
estranged by
a disappeared adolescence
eye lashed from rain
now inside the public library
unaware of other patrons
always asking for paper
sitting forever
reading art books
(as a future cognoscenti)
from celestial shelves
of expressionism.

# *RAIN*

Rain has kept us indoors
from our zen garden
the water rises
in Good Harbor
my shadow still fishes
on my open boat
for haddock and oysters
my fishing line
is felt all afternoon,
words engulf my consciousness
and we celebrate
the large cache for dinner.

## INDICATIONS

Not expecting
fragrances
of lilacs this early
forgiving every leaf
of regret for another day
with a dry mouth memory
of a fully born death
on the obituary pages
receding from view,
sneaking into a matinee
on a double featured
Japanese film festival
watching others reconciled
to a life playing ski ball
near the spliced projector.

## SOMNAMBULIST POET

Into the lamplight
reading Flaubert
embarrassingly so
as the hours dance
along my day bed
with the same chapter
and my weary French
needs a dictionary,
as the cat next door
stares at the water lily
under the still life
of a Cezanne print,
and almonds fall
from the card table
full of solitaire,
it starts to rain
the windows hear
taps on the roof
and breathless showers
from unarmed trees
on an insomniac night.

## COMPLETING APRIL'S MANUSCRIPT

Behind the backgrounds
of memoir escapes
the poet cries silently
in the hemispheric streets
asking to be spared
the hallucinogenic genes
of unconscious scrawling
slashed from a memory
of misfortune
yet knowing everything
which no one will suspect
is a spy for nature's two timers,
once seeing Timothy Leary
donning a camel skin coat
by Harvard Square
(or was it was a day dream)
in an unrecognized lotus
position hiding
like his buttonhole
falls by the newsstand

amused at a happening
at the Charles river's edge
not apologizing
for a destiny devoid
of any renewing proverbial
enlightenments
a time within time
when this poet heeds Virgil
as a backwater guide
of undiscovered reflections.

## APRIL 30TH

Wounded first light
against my skin
playing in a recital
expecting to second guess
what was locked up
inside my ink blot of notes
from my prodigy fingers
which will play
the Rain sonata
by rosin memory.

# MAY

## MAY DAY (FOR MAYAKOVSKY)

Your threadbare overcoat
is off narrowing dawn
along the Neva,
questioning the sky
on you rests
the graphic hurts
of your misgivings
in quarterly speech
prompting to ignite
a collage of high jacked
suspended consciences
to front range of Moscow's
storms of gray lifetimes
to a confronting index
and roll back the syllables
of all former vertical words
from double minded
jump started Philistines
hiding in floorboard caves
to take you out

when your own intentions
have altered your soul
into the assassin implanted
within.

## My Contemporaries

Interrupting
a bum chess game
under the elms
no one estimating
my penned in age
they call me
Shakespeare
as I walk away
with pocket money.

## PICTURES AT AN EXHIBITION

Reconciled with a branch
of an aspen a small bird
not allergic to spring water
over greensward fields
somehow not expecting
this city grackle out of tune
to sit with me hearing
"Pictures at an Exhibition."

## Not Knowing

Not knowing how to run
by the outline of my April's
new novella running wild
as jonquils cover my feet
yet in custody to words
completing my moment
of new wave fiction
as a store bought turtle
slides by my street(wise to)
my carrying a new abstract
with no will power
propitious ,as nothing dies.

## *When Endless Elegies*

When endless elegies
or quick passions
ride your imperatives
and you suddenly stop
making puzzles of it all
as melancholy winds
try to weave stolen tales
in an empire's dreams
not suited to you
or when you are tied up
by an embalmed stained
wine glasses you still praise
or a year of disappointments
tries to make you crawl
in a suffocating underground
knowing every catch phrase
has a lens to dazzle the sun
in your fields back yard
Auden once told me
in a no uncertain world

of a word,
"Forget the dervishes
spun in a human heart ache
or the shy recommendations
of a career's perspective,
rather turn your head
to your good natured
attraction ,keep on entr'acte."

'

## WITH MY INITIALS

With my initials
nailed by dark green
doors,
yet the poet
is not at home
but on a hammock
as a bed rock
writing between rose
garden walls
his hair windswept
after the rain
expecting a landscape
of current words
to overturn
all phantasms of language.

## BLINDFOLD EMBRACES

A lunar landscape
mulling over a mountain
of silent music
hanging out
among stars
like hunted fur animals
over half- crazed hills
on saga dreams
in an Icelandic blanket
hiding in circling nets
from ditch waters
refusing to imitate mirrors
of death merchants
who rent other lives
by killing off other species
they imagine are indifferent
to themselves.

## *Practicing Bartok*

In drawn notes of so much
moulting cyclical pain,
his violin concerto vibrates
from my sight reading
on the music stand.

## ON SLEEVES

On sleeves
bandaged by decades
of unrecorded madness
the census posted encounters
with yesterday's wounds
in the nine circles
crawling slowly out
(in ex camera moments)
of Dante's underground.

# JUNE

## TWO IN JUNE

Riding an atavistic wave
hands down
on the diving boards
in sun washed
upper depth,
Long Beach combers take
off with the James Dean
t shirts and surf
into the sweaty waters
unlocked and mindless
in the mouths
of non existence.

## WIND SAILS

Off Gloucester
with the wind sails
burning up the coast
that tomorrow's red sun
disappears at first light,
my brow beaten
into a Melville frenzy
spotting a Big White
of flesh
that old Ahab
would harpoon
daring to take
a photo with enough
space and time
in these storm clouds
before a voyage landing,
and the breeze taking
even the crows
on the home harbor's neck.

# JULY

## BY A JULY STATUE

Burgeoning revolutionary
in a negative synthesis
of Hegelian spirit (with fisticuffs)
they carry you on shoulders
every twenty years
until another Napoleon
has eaten your private brunch
while you update your diary.

## JULY AFTERNOON

Chess murmurs
in low voices
ringed by pawns
she wanting to watch
for the fortieth time
"Sleepless in Seattle"
the elements
were not with us
now she demands to know
if her descendants survived
the shrugs of centuries
as time flies rain
on her limpid eyebrows
in petulant speculation.

## BREATHING OUT

By tall grass and grove
on Boston Common
by revolutionary graves
history is always drained
in the Frog Pond's
a memory of sparrows
springs out from my mouth
on once uneven headstones
with a flicker of curled up
familiar desire
hearing a drinking song
from the tavern nearby
the marathon.

## THREE CUPS

Some nights pass
with three cups of wine
pass my trembling hands
hot as dog days
suddenly falls
over the devil's wharf
filled with hungry feral cats
near the marble steps
of the jazz club
my shoelaces are gone
as an explosion
from my car
reminds me my bills
terrorizing any constraint
of self-pitying misfortune
to plunge us (quickly)
into depression
braying like a lost mule
and makes the serpent
of a malignant attitude
trying play catch-up

with this double minded
blushing poor in the mouth
of a once gutsy guy
putting my used car
in reverse, like the verse
of  impossibilities
not believing this night
as sirens sound
bathing us in sweat
is all due to my expletives
by tasting the French wine
of a skeptical oration
from an enriched Beat poet.

## HIGH JACKED

On the aviary
a bird song sirens
in the cloudy airless
at atmospheric shadows
blips in a hovering space
of western blue angels
having a chilling air show
by transformers of radar
not knowing the echoes
transmitting on the sea
or alive by land marks
Jack always friendly
from a California sky
falls a million miles
on his feet.

# AUGUST

## LASSITUDE

Enough of weariness
we demand floodlights
to pierce
our shadows
against the sun
when waters draw us
out of our shades
of uprootedness
and smash oceans
of heavy icons with a Russian breath
of winter's prey
and sleep suffers
our psyche
to pocket our ironies
and embrace loneliness
when nothing leaves us
except
myth
to escort
our thunderous Mars
seize our nerve endings

erase mirrors
of lethargic scars
to wave on the sea
turning ourselves
into mid-summer dreams.

## *August 30th, Kansas*

A town's bivouac
after nature's earthquake
rains in chimeras
on far location head winds
losing consciousness
as the radio reporter
charts mirrors of sky
having not much time
and you under a shield
by tinted glass windows
of your car breaking away
from the suicide forecast
as a staggered thunder
of impromptu fire drills
masks the charred quiet.

# SEPTEMBER

## SEPTEMBER LABOR DAY

In a hard working mill
ages back when labor
is now nomadic
not habited, invisible
as this verse is silent
industry has gone global
sabotaged to shadows
you cling to sunlight
what is memory.

## WHEN TAKING YOUR LEAVE

When taking your leave
in September's watch
the long sky spits out showers
in reverie of time
steps on a shapeless blue
umbrella over hillsides
by coils of mountain climbers
in the Rockies sunshine
meditating on stone.

## *VERMONT TOURIST*

Headlights search
for JD. Salinger
in a local coffee shop
buttonholing everyone
who has a resemblance
to a high creative I.Q.
trying to recover adolescence.

## PARIS, TEXAS

Wanting a croissant
somewhere in town
the visiting professor
of French unmatched on
his thesis on Pierre Reverdy
in a sphere of confluence
but is lost at the cafe
among cowboy tall hats
and hamburger helpers
after the good service
on an October morning.

# BY TAOS, NEW MEXICO

Wanting to read over
D.H. Lawrence's spirit
strangled by phantoms
of creative style,
all desires must pass
by Taos's sunlit roads
encircled by landscapes
among ancestral voices
from painters on rocks.

## PLAYING MOZART IN PRAGUE

My hand understudies
in a universal chair
my fingers ready
for every cadenza
to play on a freelancing noon
with a travel map
inside my arm's modesty
making notes beat alive
in an aesthetically suited
augmented position
after the Prague spring
admits us to sidewalks
with outstretched applause
in energy's sunlight
leaving scales and footprints
scattered as signed programs
from eyewitnesses
initialed for scores
of open air crowds, bedraggled

in traffic with bravos freelancing
by rush hour motor cars.

## At Summer's End

at whirling ebb tide
an acrobatic dancer
asks for a partner
   a glass harmonica
responds
on an uneasy voyage
climate
changes  our field notes
brass band open
in a delectable cadenza
sounding of fragments
A flat  arpeggios
swirls the channels
and you play alto sax
with your crushed thumb
to the current improvisations
with high notes of opinion.

# OCTOBER

## OCTOBER 12TH

Magnetic sky music
embraces unknown
hemispheres scales
augmented to oblivion
of planetary muses
on retrospective spheres
open mouthed
from twelve tones
of Busoni
here in my poet's chair
disarmed with printed
cutting room edges
punctured film scores
of integrated art
supplying the stars
with voices, mirages
images, in a chorus line
before one can say
Minnesota.

## OCTOBER 20TH

They called me
Shakespeare
when my absurdist
plays were off, off
Broadway's strip
in a young cast
of fractured hopes
the critics acting
out wordless flesh
to our alembic locution.

## OCTOBER 30TH

Unguarded owl hours
words inconvenient
yet powerful in red eyed
buzz in a city minute
by a home harbor
on gas lit esplanades
the birds rest on
a latitude's gazebo
as transparent winds
in the delirium's regatta
as a port call on my cell
when riderless swimmers
race on the Charles River.

# NOVEMBER

## COUNTING WORDS

Counting words
for sci fi fiction
siphoning off a beer
by a coast cafe
near the Aquarium
listening to Bach
outside Pacific bluffs
from waves in a riotous sea
putting on a sweat shirt
under an orange umbrella
in a somnambulist rain
with city rumors
on my runaway time
of a tsunami
getting integrated
into my friendly kayak
on ocean counterpoints
of no return.

## DOWN ON HIS LUCK

November is always
off the record or road wise
driving out West
by windy street corners
seeking directions,
poor mouthed at dawn
no one putting coins
on my eyes as yet
he picks up
another four seasoned
refugee, once a stunt
and a light show guy
betrayed by the darkness
of a passed war's routine
no upstart or stand up
comedian any more,
he's reconciled with art
and only trembles
in first auditions for a bit
outstretched by silence

asks for a hand out
on the bridge
to nowhere.

## WATER SHORTAGE

Rates of statistics
from catastrophic
climate critics
not listened to;
upon the mountain
a mother and child
under shadows of trees;
only drops of rain.

## *METAMORPHOSES*

Day has lost
an echo of sleep
combing through
metamorphoses
with nature's face,
breathing on
a fully grown ash,
vying with winds
under the sun's eye,
shadowing stone
abandoned by memory.

# DECEMBER

## DECEMBER MEMOIR

His life sentence:
walking the Beat
for his conviction
that art will outlive
my transport stalled
in the Nevada desert
crossing by a no go area
the sun goes in
cross country
a move from a sponged fog
by a sorry shade
of black and blue denim
as a lifeless cactus
feeling ashen and low rise
on an insomniac day
common as hazelnuts
pins down
all poetic opprobrium.

## SEMBLANCE

Unwinding language
being shy
for the cameras

over this metropolis
with words
in an attaché case

holding my words
for an urban read
held by four strings

(near wrinkled chords
of my travel guitar)
convulsed by warmth

mirrored as rain
for a runaway time
such as this,

facing a Beat poet's
blindfolded awareness
you may yet recognize

him or an age trembling
to split in two shards
of memory's enlightenment.

## *EVERYTHING, EVERYWHERE*

Inspired by mangroves
of intertwined mesh dreams
clothing your sleep
on your unmarked door
lost to easy streets
making your universe
   out of stone hedges
in the underground art scene
(where rivers of rock
move from the pack iced sea
and indigo bars
of axletrees on wheels)
informing your cosmic dust
of imagination's inspection
you carve a preoccupation
for dazzling headless beauty
in sunshine's paradigm
now living in a lost
nature of shadows
of three dimensional sculpture

whose only presence
are unfinished heliotropes
broken in for art's sake.

## *About The Author*

B.Z. NIDITCH is a
poet, playwright,
and fiction writer.

His work is widely
published in journals
and magazines
throughout the
world, including: Columbia: A Magazine of
Poetry and Art; The Literary Review;
Denver Quarterly; Hawaii Review; Le
Guepard (France); Kadmos (France); Prism
International; Jejune (Czech Republic);
Leopold Bloom (Hungary); Antioch
Review; and Prairie Schooner, among
others. His latest poetry collections are
"Lorca at Seville" and "Captive Cities."

He lives in Brookline, Massachusetts.

## ABOUT THE COVER ARTIST

Sarah Katharina Kayss is winner of the manuscript-award of the German Writers Association for her poetry and essay collection Ich mag die Welt, so wie sie ist (Allitera: Munich 2014) and works on her doctorate in military sociology at King's College London. Her artwork, essays and poetry have appeared in literary magazines, journals and anthologies in Germany, Switzerland, Austria, the United Kingdom, Italy, Canada, New Zealand and the United States.

www.SarahKatharinaKayss.com

## PREVIOUSLY PUBLISHED WORKS

- <u>Somnambulist Poet</u>, rapoetics.com, 6/24/2012<u>Expectations (for Tomas Tranströmer)</u>, Randomly Accessed Poetics, No. 1, Texture of Words, 2012
- <u>With My Initials</u>, rapoetics.com, 10/7/2012
- <u>Lamentations</u>, Randomly Accessed Poetics, No.2, Paint Darkness Into Day, 2012
- <u>Waiting</u>, Randomly Accessed Poetics, No. 4, Heart Splatters Into Significance, 2013
- <u>Three Cups</u>, Randomly Accessed Poetics, No. 4, Heart Splatters Into Significance, 2013
- <u>At Summer's End</u>, Randomly Accessed Poetics, No. 4, Heart Splatters Into Significance, 2013
- <u>Love's Self Deceptions</u>, rapoetics.com, 2/9/2014
- <u>Semblance</u>, Randomly Accessed Poetics, No.5, Anti-Photonic Illumination, 2014
- <u>Water Shortage</u>, rapoetics.com, 1/18/2015
- <u>Rain</u>, Randomly Accessed Poetics, No. 6, Ghost House, 2015
- <u>Wind Sales</u>, rapoetics.com, 5/17/2015

## MORE FROM PENHEAD PRESS

**The Color Red Does Not Sleep**. Poetry by Dawnell Harrison. Cover art by Dion Loubser. Penhead Press Chapbook Series No. 1

**In The Soup: Demented Recipes 2009 - 2014.** Flash fiction works by Carla Blaschka. Cover art by William J. Lindberg. Penhead Press Chapbook Series No. 2

**Found on Bathroom Walls.** Poetry, prose, photography, and cover art by William James Lindberg. Penhead Press Chapbook Series No. 3

These books and more can be found on Amazon.com

**Randomly Accessed Poetics, No. 6: Ghost House.** Contains poetry, prose, and art by Carrie Albert, Pratima Annapurna Balabhadrapathruni, Robert Bates, Matthew Lane Brouwer, John Burgess, Dennis Caswell, Joanna Conom, Larry Crist, Holly Day, B.Z. Niditch, and many more